Circle the animals that aren't from Africa.

Answers

Asian elephant

Golden lion tamarin

Lowland paca

Finish drawing the octopus.

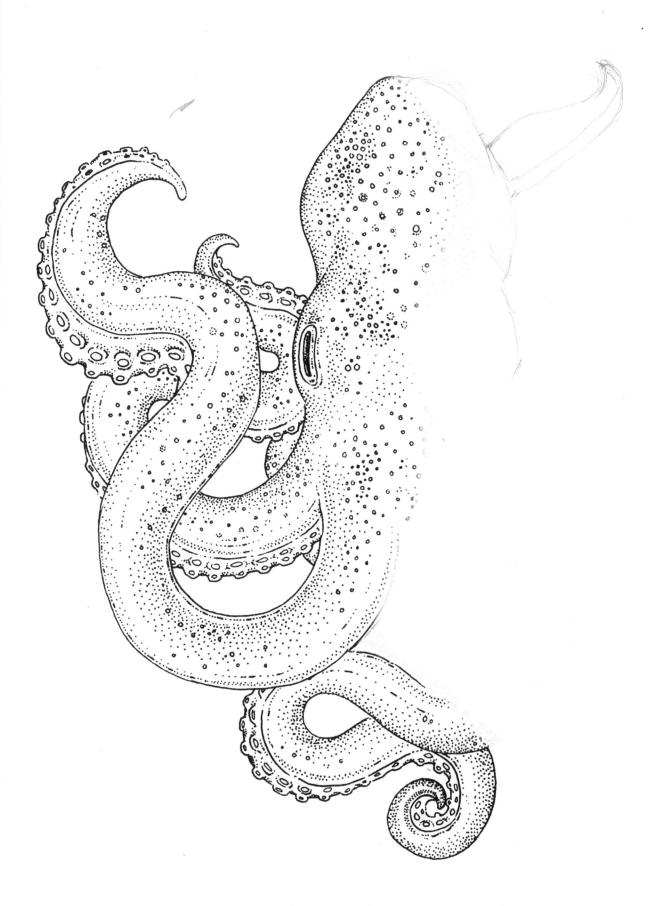

Angel octopus

Velodona togata
Mantle: 6 inches/15 centimeters
This deep-sea octopus lives at depths of up to 2,000 feet/700 meters.

Add more frogs
to this rain-forest habitat.

Examples of rain-forest frogs

Blue poison-dart frog

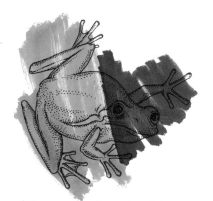

Waxy monkey leaf frog

Granular poison-dart frog

Match the animal pairs.

There are invertebrates, amphibians, and birds.

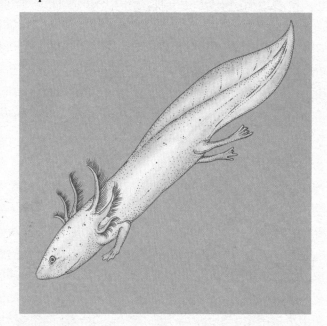

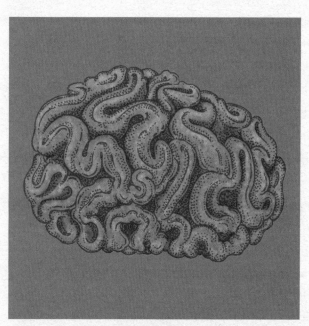
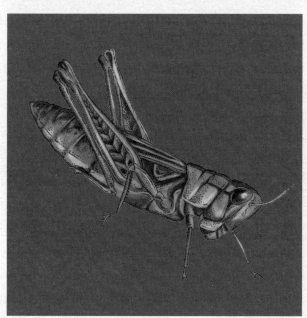

Answers

The brain coral and green grasshopper are both invertebrates.

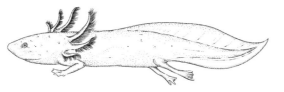 

The axolotl and Allen's worm salamander are both amphibians.

The bateleur and ruby-topaz hummingbird are both birds.

How to draw a lion

1
2
3
4

Try it yourself.

Lion

Panthera leo
Length: 9.3 feet/2.9 meters
Second only to the tiger in size, this big cat is
immediately recognizable thanks to its mane. It lives in
prides where the females hunt together for food.

Add animals to this coastal habitat.

Some coastal habitat creatures

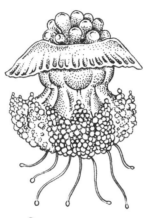

Crown jellyfish

Calico scallop

Cushion star

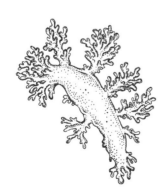

Bushy-backed sea slug

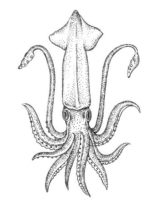

Northern short-fin squid

Label the parts of the fish.

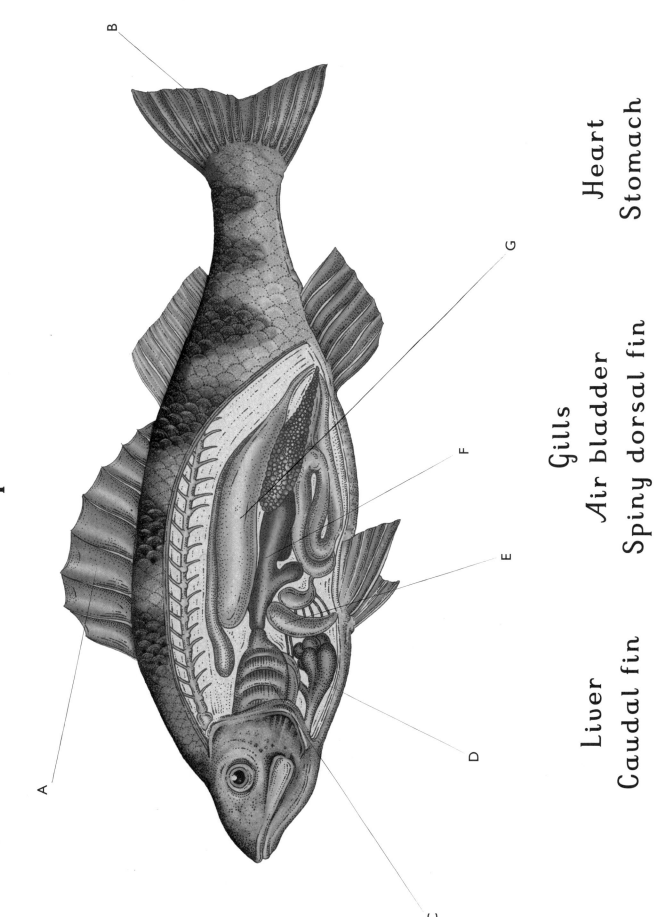

A

B

C

D

E

F

G

Liver   Gills   Heart

Caudal fin   Air bladder   Stomach

               Spiny dorsal fin

Answers

A: Spiny dorsal fin
B: Caudal fin
C: Gills
D: Heart
E: Liver
F: Stomach
G: Air bladder

Circle the matching pair of ornate horned frogs.

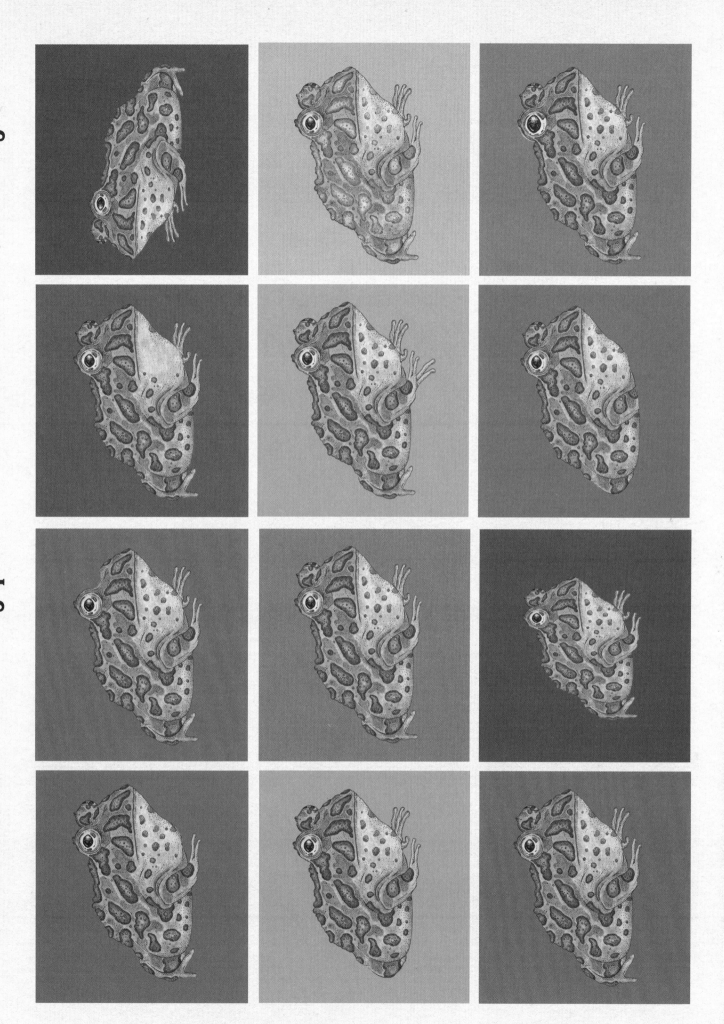

Answer

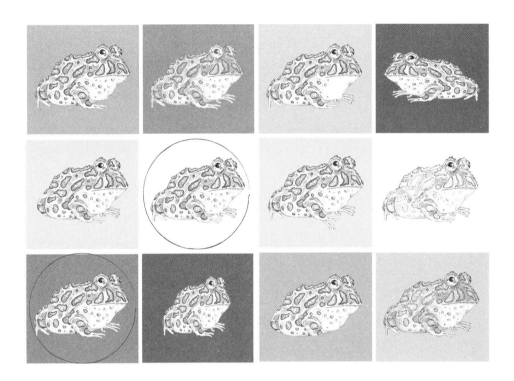

Complete the flying insects.

Examples of flying insects

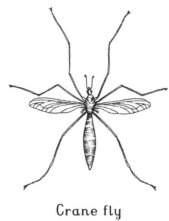

Crane fly

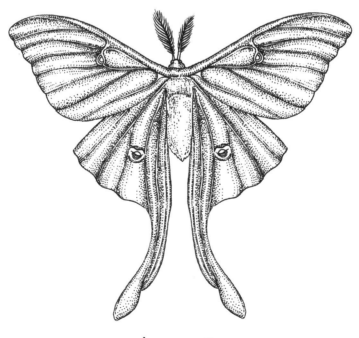

Luna moth

Color the
desert scene.

Baja California collared lizard

Crotaphytus vestigium
Body length: 3½ inches/9 centimeters
This creature hibernates under a rock in the cold winter months
and becomes active in the warmer seasons. When running, it can
become bipedal, standing up on its two hind legs.

Put these animals in order according to their true size, with 1 being the smallest and 8 the largest.

Answers

1. Common wasp: 1/2 inch/1.5 centimeters
2. Granular poison-dart frog: 1 inch/2.5 centimeters
3. Ruby-topaz hummingbird: 3 inches/8 centimeters
4. Luna moth: 4 inches/10 centimeters
5. Emperor penguin: 3 feet/1 meter
6. Green sea turtle: 5 feet/1.5 meters
7. Spotted eagle ray: 6 feet/1.8 meters
8. Humpback whale: 46 feet/14 meters

Create your own exotic bird.

Exotic birds

Ruby-throated hummingbird

Ruby-topaz hummingbird

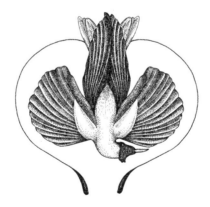

Greater bird-of-paradise

Help the clownfish escape
the jellyfish maze.

Finish

Answer

Color the butterfly and moth.

Blue Mormon butterfly

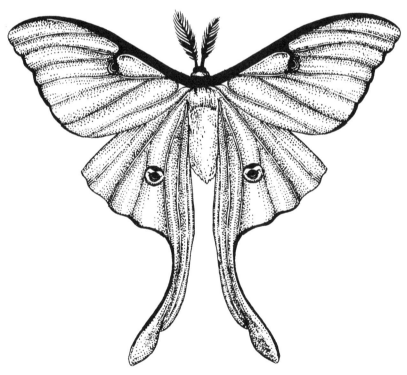

Luna moth

Add more snakes
to the tangle.

Snakes

Snakes are characterized by their lack of limbs and their long, tube-like
bodies. They are believed to have descended from lizards, losing their
limbs in the process of evolution.

Spot the differences.

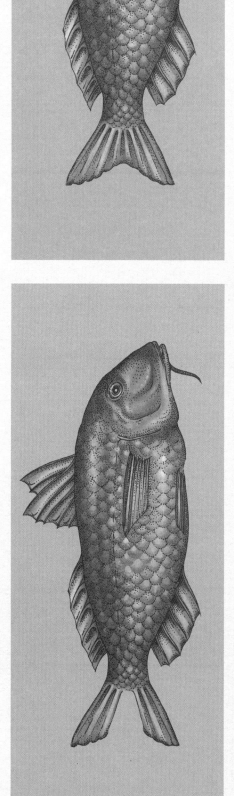

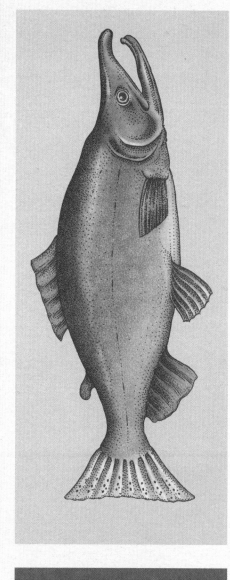

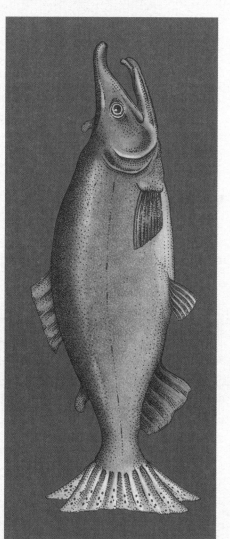

Answers

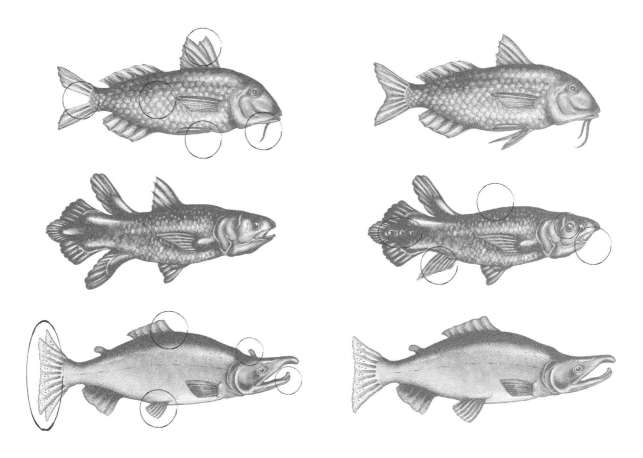

Create your own bat face.

 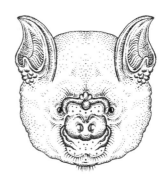

Bats

There are more than 900 recognized bat species. Bats
are the only mammals that have evolved to fly. They are
mostly nocturnal creatures, sleeping through the day
and coming out to hunt at twilight.

Label the parts of the crocodile skeleton.

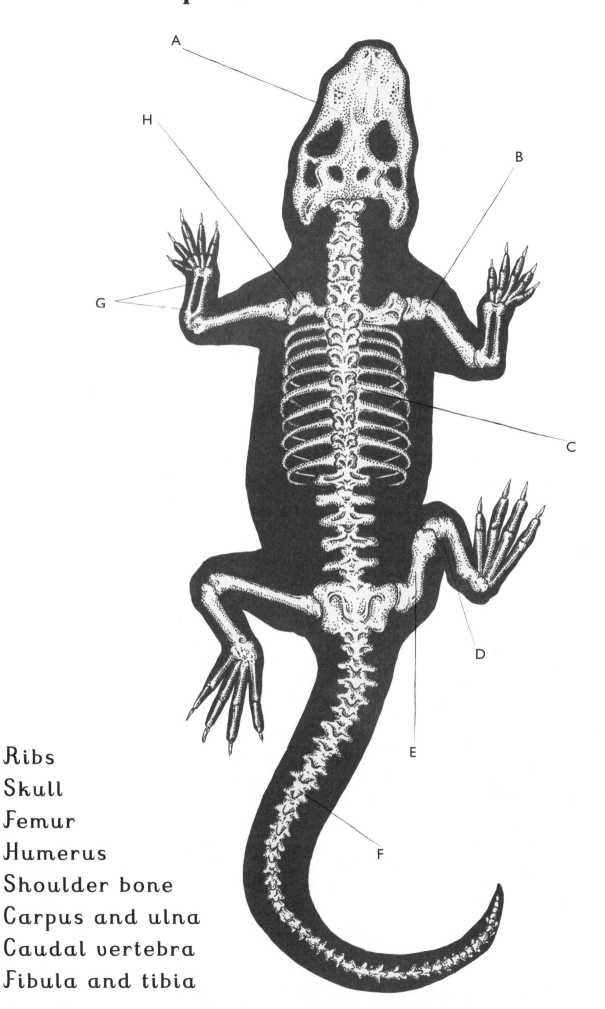

Ribs
Skull
Femur
Humerus
Shoulder bone
Carpus and ulna
Caudal vertebra
Fibula and tibia

Answers

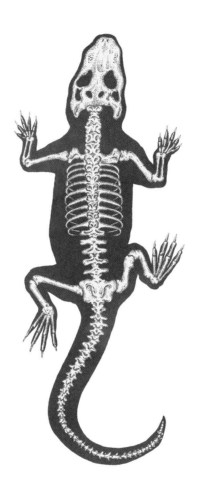

A. Skull
B. Humerus
C. Ribs
D. Fibula and tibia
E. Femur
F. Caudal vertebra
G. Carpus and ulna
H. Shoulder bone

Add an emperor
penguin chick.

Emperor penguin

Aptenodytes forsteri
Height: 3 feet/1 meter
The emperor penguin is famous for its
reproductive cycle. It breeds during
the Antarctic winter between May and June, when
no other creature inhabits the region, which
reduces the threat of predators. The female then departs,
leaving the male to incubate the egg by balancing
it on his feet. He must survive more than three months
without any food until the female returns.

Add wings to these insects.

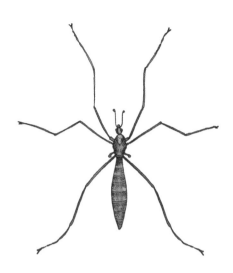

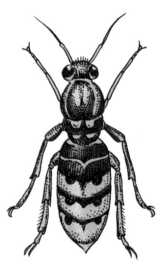

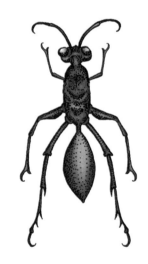

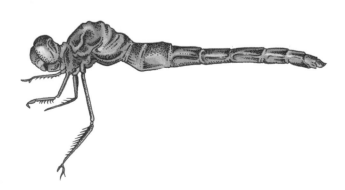

Insects with wings

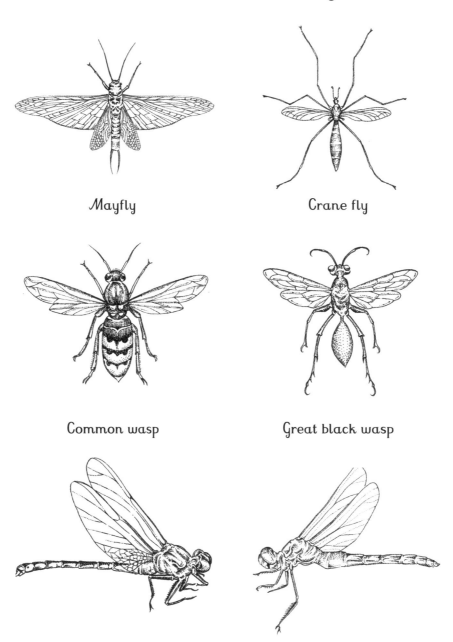

Mayfly

Crane fly

Common wasp

Great black wasp

Emperor dragonfly

Pale snaketail dragonfly

Use the grid to draw a caracara.

Crested caracara

Crested caracara

Caracara plancus
Wingspan: 4 feet/1.2 meters
The crested caracara is found in open land in the southern
parts of North America through Peru and Amazonian Brazil,
and is a common sight on cattle ranches. It is not an agile
flyer and seldom hunts for prey, opting instead to scavenge
for food and feed on carrion.

Circle the predators.

Answers

Lion

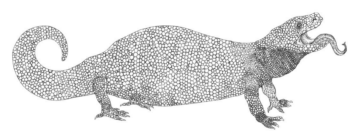

Gila monster

White's treefrog

Common wasp

This pattern is from a terrapin shell.
Fill the page by repeating the pattern.

Diamondback terrapin

Malaclemys terrapin
Length: 6 inches/15 centimeters
The mild-mannered diamondback terrapin lives in brackish
lagoons, tidal marshlands, and sandy beaches in east-coast
America. The species nearly became extinct due to over-
hunting and destruction of its habitat.

Circle the marsupials.

Answers

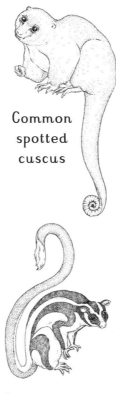

Common
spotted
cuscus

Striped possum

Sugar glider

Koala

Draw your own food chain.

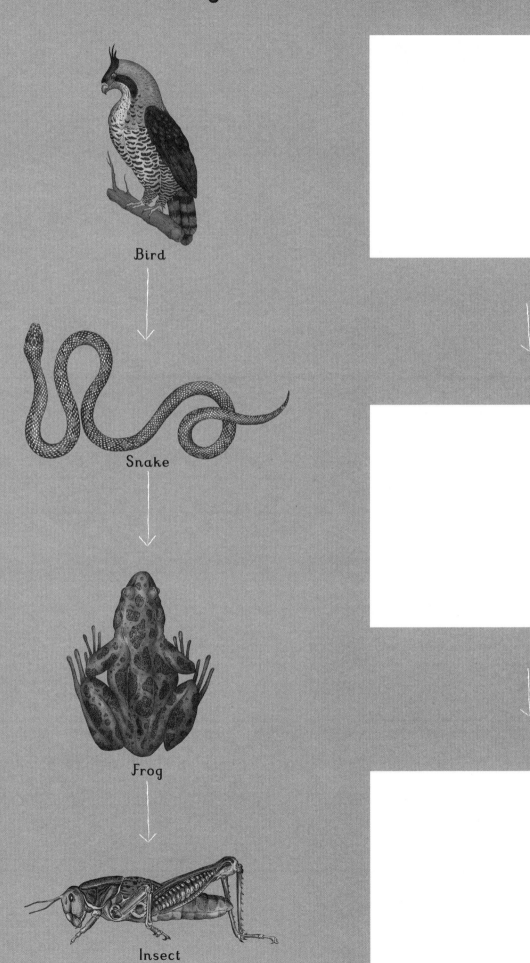

Bird

Snake

Frog

Insect

Another example of a food chain

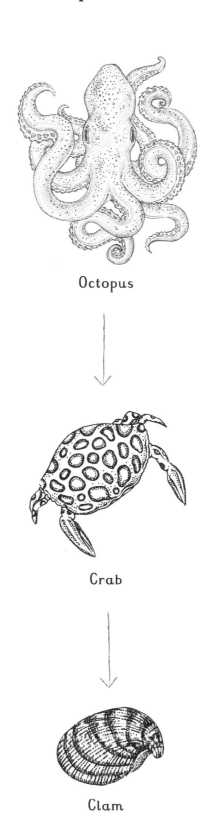

Octopus

Crab

Clam

Finish drawing the sea creatures.

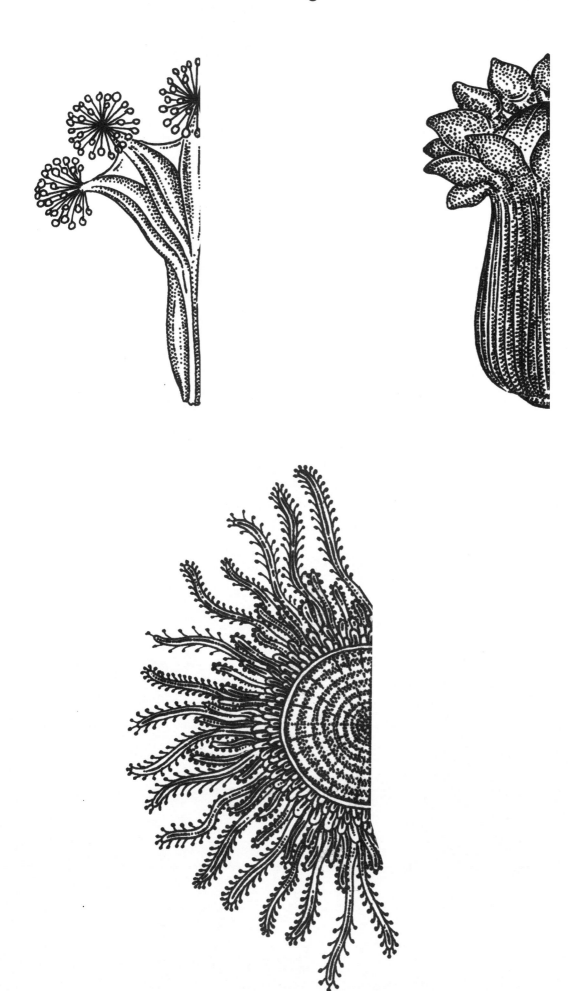

Sea creatures

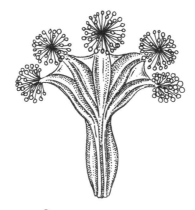

Stalked jellyfish

Blue button jellyfish

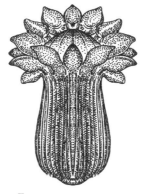

Flowerpot coral

Add fish to
this coral reef.

Examples of coral-reef fish

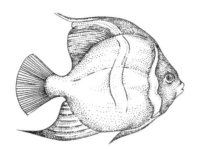

French angelfish

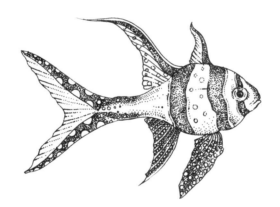

Banggai cardinalfish

Mandarinfish

Color the sea sponges.

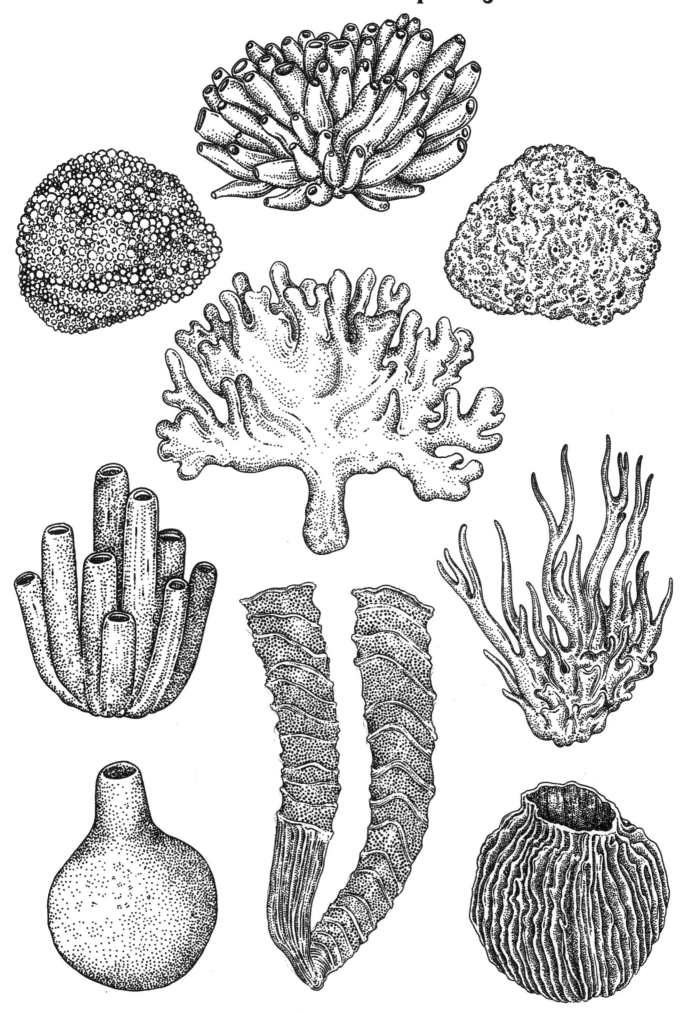

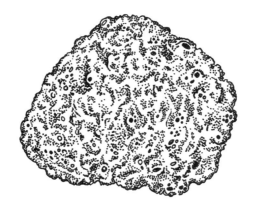

Sea sponges

Porifera, or sponges, date back to 665 million years ago. The evolution of
the multicellular sponge was one of the most significant developments in
natural history. Living exclusively underwater, sponges can be found in all
habitats, from tropical seas to icy waters.

Fill in the giraffe's spots.

Masai giraffe

Giraffa camelopardalis tippelskirchi
Height: 18 feet/5.5 meters
The African Masai giraffe is the tallest land mammal on Earth.
Its long legs and neck have evolved to allow it to feed from the
treetops, and its long and flexible tongue extends to gather twigs
and leaves. When competing for a mate, males duel by battering
one another with their long necks.

Use the grid to draw the ray.

Thornback ray

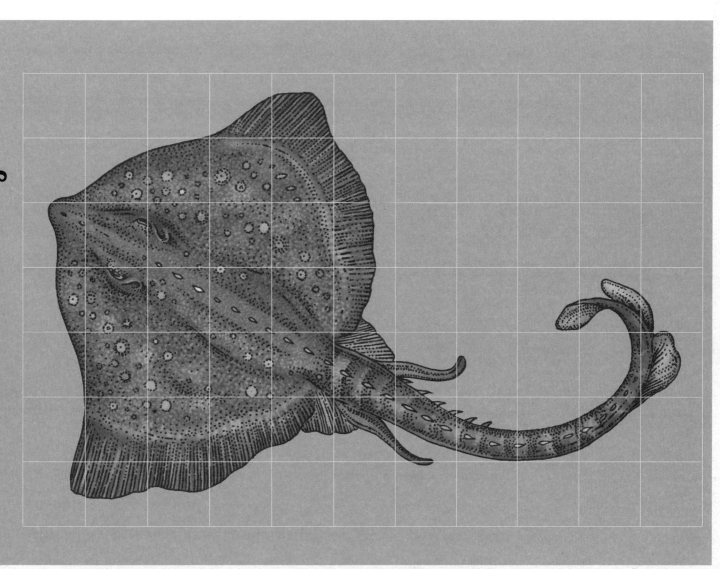

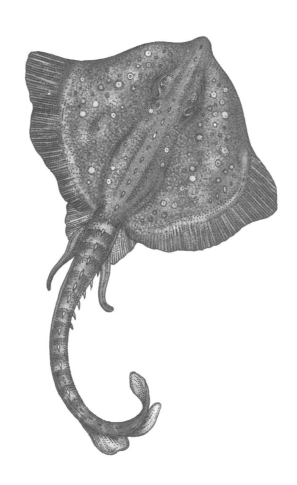

Thornback ray

Raja clavata
Length: 33 inches/85 centimeters
This kite-shaped ray is one of the most commonly seen species, although it
can be difficult to identify because coloration varies from
fish to fish. It has between thirty-six and forty-four rows of teeth in its
upper jaw, and its long, solid tail has thorns running down its length.

Spot the differences.

Answers

How to draw an elephant

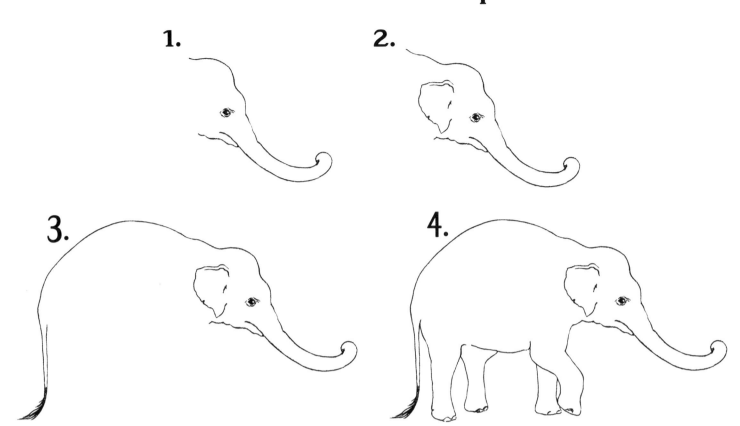

1.

2.

3.

4.

Try it yourself.

Asian elephant

Elephas maxiumus
Height: 8 1/2 feet/2.6 meters
The Asian elephant has smaller ears and a more arched back than its African cousins. It also has smaller tusks, if it has any at all. Both types of elephants are instantly recognizable by their long flexible trunks, which they use to grab and hold objects, and their large, flat ears.

Match the animal pairs.

There are amphibians, mammals, and reptiles.

Answers

The White's treefrog and Mandarin salamander are both amphibians.

The de Brazza's monkey and Weddell
seal are both mammals.

The Gila monster and leopard tortoise are both reptiles.

Draw the stages of the frog and moth life cycles.

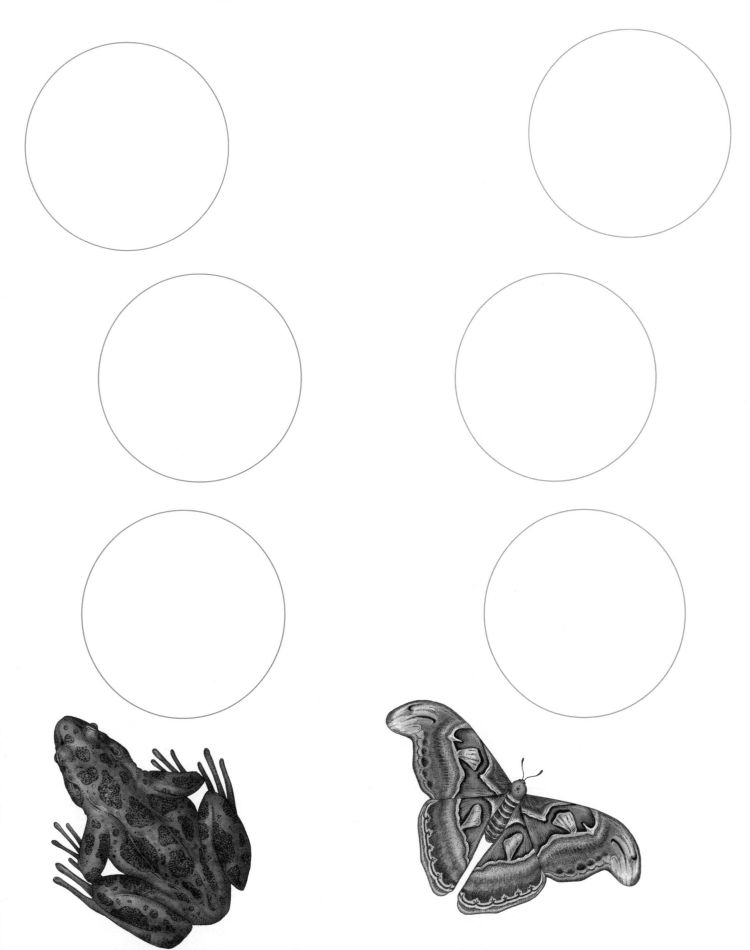

Answers

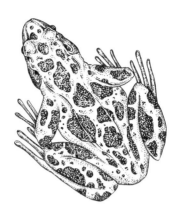

Frogspawn	Egg
↓	↓
Tadpole	Caterpillar
↓	↓
Froglet	Cocoon
↓	↓
Frog	Moth

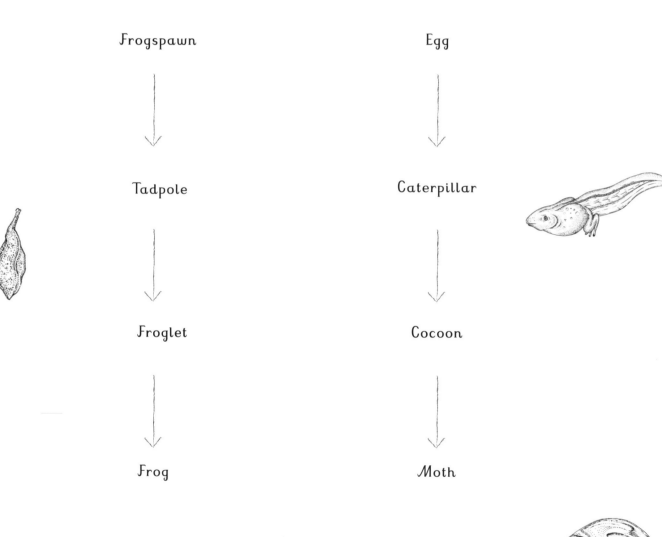

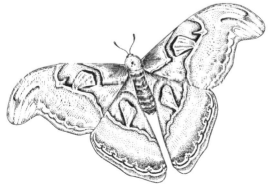

Finish drawing the animals.

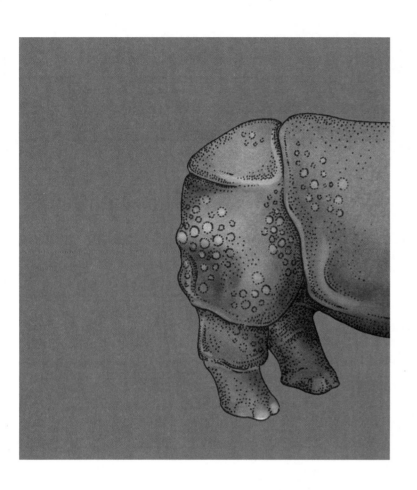

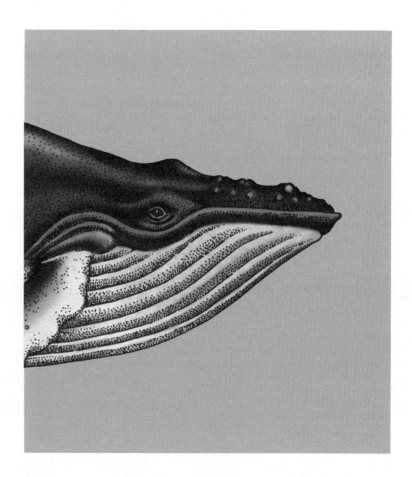

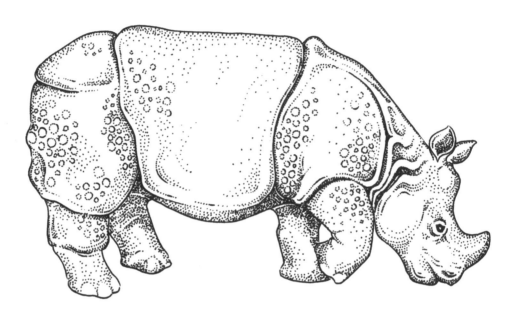

Indian rhinoceros

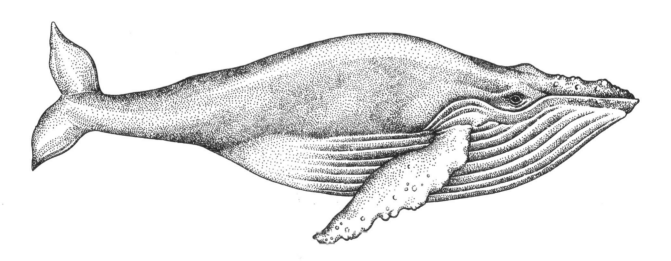

Humpback whale